100+

QUESTIONS

That Lead Teams to Build Smart, Aggressive Project Plans

Version 3.0

ALAN WILLETT and **JULIA MULLANEY**

Alan Willett

Expert consultant, speaker, and award-winning author of **Lead With Speed** and **Leading the Unleadable;** *How to Manage Cynics, Divas, and Other Difficult People*. Alan Willett is co-founder of Exceptional Difference. Alan works with clients around the world solving problems for organizations large and small.

Julia Mullaney

With a commitment to changing the world of software engineering, Julia Mullaney, co-founder of Exceptional Difference, is an award-winning engineer, instructor, leader, and consultant who has worked with software companies in many industries across the globe.

Exceptional Difference

Over the past two decades, the Exceptional Difference team has proven that software-intensive system development doesn't have to be a painful process full of unknowns. Our unique approach cuts to the core of the problems in a way that traditional training and consulting cannot.

We help organizations achieve results they never thought possible. The organizations we work with begin to keep (or beat) every commitment they make, deliver high-quality products, eliminate costly rework, and more. They see incredible changes in company culture thanks to a new-found trust and harmony between the team and management.

About the Field Guide Series

The Field Guide Series emulates the tradition where experts share their real-world experience in the form of a book filled with practical wisdom, helping others survive and thrive in the challenging wildness of the world.

Exceptional Difference field guides provide readers with practical information they can use to solve immediate, real-world problems.

"As has been taught to teachers of the Harvard Business School, the art of asking good questions is often the most important element of managerial tasks."

Parte Bose

100+ QUESTIONS

That Lead Teams to Build Smart, Aggressive Project Plans

Version 3.0

Project teams should build smart, aggressive plans that enable them to make commitments to their management and, ultimately, their customers. A smart plan is well thought out to provide the quickest, high-value option possible. Being quick should always be paired with commitments the team can keep and even beat.

We have found again and again that teams build plans and deliver results based on the questions that leaders ask. For example, one vice president repeatedly asked software developers to "hurry up and get the software to testers so they could start finding the defects." The developers, of course, obliged, and the testers found so many defects it took twice as long in development to find and fix enough of them to deliver a working product.

Building smart plans quickly with low effort requires leadership to ask the questions that drive the kind of results you want. In other words, this book of questions was created to set and reinforce expectations of excellence in the teams that build your products.

The questions overlap on purpose. We expect you to vary the questions to keep your teams thinking. Over multiple project reviews, ask the right questions in as many ways as possible.

Please add your own situational awareness and judgment for any project plan review. We expect you to customize the questions for your project, eliminate irrelevant questions, and be sure to ask questions not listed here that are critical to you and your organization.

> "The manager asks how and when; the leader asks what and why."
>
> Warren Bennis

Customer Focus

All projects have a customer, but often there is both a project customer and an end user of the product. Too often, teams lose focus on the end customer. It could be that there are too many steps or people between the project team and that customer or that the team is distracted by shiny new technology. Whatever the cause, asking questions like the following will ensure the project team has a clear understanding of the customer and their needs.

01. Describe your customer's most important needs from their point of view.

02. What experiences do team members have in the customer domain?

03. Who on the team has met with customers or used the products or services the customer uses? Describe the experience.

04. Why will the results of this project be useful to the customer? What value will they get?

05. How would a representative customer use the results of this project?

06. What is the most important attribute of this project? Is it content, cost (including staffing), or schedule?

07. What external milestones or events are driving the project schedule?

08. Describe the minimally valuable product. With what points would a customer agree or disagree?

09. If the product is released in versions, what is the release schedule and how is the schedule determined?

10. How will the customer(s) be supported in the first weeks of using the new features?

11. How will the customer determine whether their needs have been met with this product?

12. How will the team ensure the product is meeting customer needs?

Key Point: Make sure the team is not delusional about customer needs. The team should be able to state their assumptions about the customer's needs and explain how they will meet them.

Project Dependencies

No project exists in a vacuum, yet many project plans make that assumption. Repeatedly I have seen project plans that were fine except for this key aspect, but like the Titanic with its assumptions, the projects sunk. Your questions here will make sure the team is thinking through any external issues they may face.

13. How does this project relate to other projects in the organization? Are there other projects dependent upon this one, and conversely, are there projects this project is dependent upon?

14. Which dependencies are most likely to put the project at risk?

15. For dependencies most likely to put the project at risk, what mitigation and contingency plans has the team put in place?

16. How and how often is the team monitoring schedule dependencies? Who is responsible for that task?

17. How is the team communicating with other projects about these dependencies?

18. What alternatives has the team considered that could eliminate or reduce dependencies?

19. Which team members have significant responsibilities outside of this project? What is the relative priority of other responsibilities compared to this project?

20. Are there team members who are working part-time on this project? If so, how is their available time calculated and tracked?

21. If you could magically eliminate one dependency, what would it be and what would you gain by eliminating it?

Key Point: In complex systems, dependencies are often a bottleneck to progress. It's important that teams identify dependencies up front and are proactive about managing those dependencies throughout the project.

"One of the true tests of leadership is the ability to recognize a problem before it becomes an emergency."

Arnold Glasow

"The alternative to good design is always bad design. There is no such thing as no design."

Adam Judge

Smart and Fast

When managers push teams because their estimates are too high, they lead teams to make smaller estimates. The Gantt charts may look better, but the dates become fiction. Managers should make sure the team has considered the best ways to shorten the schedule in reality. These questions will help the team to design a development strategy in a smart, fast way.

22. How many design approaches did the team consider? Why did they agree on a particular design approach?

23. Who's reviewed the design?

24. What design methods are the team using?

25. How much time is being spent in design compared to implementation and testing?

26. What could management do to help the project/team go faster?

27. What other people or skills added to the team would help the project go faster?

28. Are there third-party components that should be licensed/purchased to enable faster completion?

29. What assistance can management provide to help the team be more productive?

30. What defect-removal techniques are the team using? How is the team measuring their effectiveness?

31. What software assets can be reused to improve project speed without negatively impacting quality?

32. What short cuts are being taken to increase speed that will also increase technical debt? Are they worth it? Why?

33. What are three key things leadership could provide to help accelerate the project?

Key Point: There are two common ways to drive from San Francisco to LA. The scenic but slow Route 1, or the expressway. Make sure your team has considered both options, as well as other options, such as taking an airplane, chartering a jet, or just staying in San Francisco and making a phone call.

"The conventional definition of management is getting work done through people, but real management is developing people through work."

Agha Hasan Abedi

Building for the Future

Management is always balancing the need for short-term gains with long-term goals. These questions are designed to help you with this balance. In most organizations, management does not ask these questions and the teams do not share the shortcuts taken. Thus critical assets become rusty and the company accumulates hidden technical debt. Even worse, it's often people skills that get rusty. These questions will help you see the problems your teams are facing so that more intelligent choices can be made.

34. Is the team approach going to add to the product's technical debt or decrease it? Explain.

35. How easy will it be for the company to be able to build on the finished project for future enhancements?

36. What are the obstacles to this product becoming an asset for the company's future?

37. What software languages are being used? How large is the their user? Who provides support? What's the risk of obsolescence?

38. What support tools are being used? How large is their user base? Who provides support? What's the risk of obsolescence?

39. What skills and talents are team members developing on this project?

40. What skills and talents should team members be developing on this project?

41. In what ways is the company at risk of falling behind the pace of technology?

42. How will the team's approach build our talent assets?

43. How will the team's approach build our product assets?

Key Point: As you build your projects, the teams should also be building a set of high-quality assets. Additionally, your team should be continuously improving their skill set, which is an even more important asset.

> "Quality is never an accident.
> It is always the result of
> intelligent effort."
>
> **John Ruskin**

A Smart Focus on Quality

When we ask a room of executives if they believe removing defects early in the cycle is less expensive than removing them later, they all say yes. A focus on quality is the most effective way to reduce project costs and finish sooner, yet most project plans do not focus on quality. The following questions guide teams to plan for high quality and track as well as schedule.

44. What methods are being used to remove defects before delivery?

45. How is the team using historical data to control quality?

46. What is the expected cost of quality for this project? How was it calculated?

47. At what points in the process is the team tracking defects that were found and fixed?

48. How big is the legacy base?

49. Which modules in the legacy base have the highest defect density?

50. Has the team considered replacing the high-risk legacy modules? Why or why not?

51. How effective are the team's inspections? How do they know?

52. How many customer scenarios have been estimated? Tested?

53. How are user interface prototypes being validated with the customer?

54. What prototypes are being used for conceptual verification of new technological approaches?

55. How many defects the team calculates will remain in the product after test?

56. What are the possible (bad to worst) outcomes for the end users of our products?

57. Does the team believe it can deliver a near zero-defect product? Why or why not?

58. What can management do to help the team deliver a high-quality product?

Key Point: Delivering high-quality products quickly becomes a habit when a smart focus is applied early.

"Talent wins games, but teamwork and intelligence win championships."

Michael Jordan

A High Confidence Commitment to Schedule

These *"smart and aggressive"* questions lead to the fastest, smartest approach.

59. How does project size compare with previous projects?

60. How does the schedule compare with similar projects?

61. What methods were used to make time and schedule estimates? How granular were the estimates?

62. How is the team tracking the plan? To what level of detail?

63. How likely is it that this project will finish on schedule?

64. How many days (or weeks) of data are needed to know how accurate the estimates are?

65. How does the plan account for out-of-office times, planned or likely? *(Vacation/holidays, conferences/site visits, training, etc.)*

66. If you have rate data *(e.g. productivity)*, how does this plan compare to similar projects?

67. How many effort hours per week are planned compared to historical data?

68. How are risks/issues managed?

69. Have you accounted for plan growth due to things like missed tasks and scope creep? Is the estimated growth consistent with historical data?

70. A committed team is most likely to manage the schedule to success. Questions to help judge:

- What parts of this project are the project engineers most excited about?
- Will the project provide a good experience for the end user?
- Is the project team dedicated to delivering on their project plan commitments?

Key Point: Some executives express concern that if a team builds a conservative schedule, the team will just relax. This is a leadership issue. Teams like to win. It's best to build a conservative schedule and inspire your team deliver on-time or, better yet, early. That is the challenge of exceptional leadership.

Anticipating Change

No amount of planning will prevent the plan from changing when it meets reality. The questions in this section will lead your team to acknowledge reality, and better yet, anticipate it.

71. How much growth in requirements does the team's plan assume?

72. What requirements are most likely to change?

73. How will the team evaluate, manage, and track requirement change requests?

74. What new requirements do you anticipate to occur before project completion?

75. What other commitments do team members have that could take priority over this project *(inside or outside of work)*?

76. Which dependencies are most volatile? What interruptions do you anticipate from management?

77. What are the top risks to the project?

78. What things are you concerned about?

79. What things could go wrong?

Key Point: Teams often complain that it is hard to hit a moving target. These questions make it clear that the team's job is to anticipate a moving target. Instill this habit early by ensuring all projects start with a good plan that you have reviewed.

"It's a bad plan that admits of no modification."

Publilius Syrus

"If we have data, let's look at data. If all we have are opinions, let's go with mine."

Jim Barksdale

Seeing and Accepting Reality

Teams will consistently deliver great projects when they manage with experience, judgment and data. We give these questions with a notice of caution as well. If teams feel they will be "punished or rewarded" for answers, they will provide the data you want to see, not what is accurate and useful to the team. It is important to be aware of what your teams are ready and able to answer.

80. What project management tools are in use? What does the team like about these tools? What do they hate about them?

81. How often is the project plan updated by the team?

82. What are the barriers to having accurate project management data?

83. How do team members track task time? Is this working well for them?

84. How often does the team meet? What are the primary topics covered?

85. How often are team members reviewing their personal plans?

86. What schedule deviation would trigger a need to revise the plan?

87. What data is the team using to manage quality? How is it collected? How useful is this data to the team?

88. How does the team track defects?

89. What data is the team and management using to make their decisions?

90. What tools are the team using to capture data? What does the team like about these tools? What do they hate?

91. How does the team compare your size and effort estimates to their actual data?

Key Point: Perhaps the most important is ask your team; Are you getting the data you need to run this project well?

"In God we trust.
All others bring data."

Edward Deming

Data-Based Feedback Loops

Too many organizations complain, "We write lessons learned, we just do not read them." One of the most impactful actions an executive can take is to make sure organizational learning is part of the DNA of the project plan. Asking these questions with follow up actions will make this happen.

92. How was historical data from previous projects used when planning this project?

93. What projects are similar to this project? What problems did previous projects like this one face, and how is the team dealing with those problems?

94. How will lessons learned be captured so they will be useful for future projects?

95. How will the team capture process and product improvement suggestions throughout the project? Where will it be stored? Will others have access?

96. At what point(s) has the team scheduled time for reflection and learning? How much time?

97. What data will the team review during these times of reflection and learning?

98. How will the team provide to others the lessons learned?

99. How will the team ensure knowledge of this product is shared outside the team?

100. How does the team plan to share learning throughout the project? (Ideas could include design walkthroughs of works in progress or including external developers on inspections)

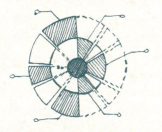

Key Point: Each of these questions should lead to short exercises that have a high return in value for the individuals and the organization.

A Plan You Believe In

Perhaps the most vital questions are for you, the leader, after you complete the project plan review.

101. Do you believe the team adequately understands the customer needs? Why?

102. Does this project fit in well with the portfolio of projects in your organization? Why?

103. Why do you believe the team has made a smart plan that will meet customer needs?

104. What talents are being developed on this team that will provide a basis for future success?

105. Will the team's output create assets for your company to build on?

106. How do you know the team's schedule is realistic?

107. How well will the team manage the pressures, challenges and changes the project will face?

108. How are you demonstrating your commitment to supporting this team in reaching a successful conclusion?

Key Point: Listen to your inner music. If you feel uncomfortable, either ask the team more questions or provide them with specific guidance on what expectations they are missing and ask them to come back with an improved plan. If you feel confident the team can meet and beat the commitments made in the plan, celebrate. Celebrate with the team.

Do you have material that you think should be added to this booklet? Send suggestions your to:

INFO@EXCEPTIONALDIFFERENCE.COM

"A clear vision, backed by definite plans, gives you a tremendous feeling of confidence and personal power."

Brian Tracy

More from the team at Exceptional Difference

EXCEPTIONAL ENGINEERING

This fully immersive experience provides the tools and training to those elite engineers whose talent and drive can change the trajectory of a team or entire organization.

EXCEPTIONAL EXECUTIVE

This program empowers highly-motivated leaders with the wisdom and tools they need to create high-performance teams, no matter the current state of the business.

DEEP DIVES

Participants gain a deep understanding of specific subject areas in high-tech systems development and an action plan to successfully implement lessons for immediate impact.

COACHING

An outside coach can make a world of difference for engineers and or managers. With the right balance of hard/tech and soft/people skills, we can help bring out the best in your top people.

CUSTOM TRAINING

Can't choose from the menu, no problem. We'll have our chef whip up something special for you and your team. Tell us what's on your mind, what's bugging you, and we'll help you construct the perfect custom training option.

CONSULTING

Sometimes you just need to pick the brains of smart people who understand where you are coming from. We can do that too. As an added bonus, we've got enough gray hair you can take us into your board room.

LEARN MORE AT EXCEPTIONALDIFFERENCE.COM

WHAT PEOPLE ARE SAYING...

"The impact on my job was almost immediate and it was pretty substantial... I was able to immediately roll out and start using what I had learned to transform how we operate here at Catchpoint."

Dylan Greiner, Chief Product Architect and Team Leader

"After the experience, my confidence is high based on the quality of my work and my ability to deliver. When I speak about project risks and the actions needed, it is no longer an argument. People engage."

Alex Powell, Software Engineer

"The Exceptional Difference series is the elite offering I was looking for. It is powering up my leaders and engineers to new heights."

Mauricio Hernandez-Distancia, Head of Central Engineering

"If you want to accelerate the growth of your key engineers and engineering leaders, the Exceptional Difference series is the accelerant you need."

Chief Engineer of Major Systems Development Program, US Navy

LEARN MORE AT EXCEPTIONALDIFFERENCE.COM

We'd love to hear from you.

Info@ExceptionalDifference.com

Notes:

Notes:

www.ingramcontent.com/pod-product-compliance
Lightning Source LLC
Chambersburg PA
CBHW041155050326
40690CB00004B/576